Coffee and Conversations

Inclusion and Belonging

by

Zenell B. Brown, Esq.

Editor: Francene Ambrose-Gunn

Author Photos: Emma Burcusel

Publisher: G Publishing LLC

ISBN: 978-1-7340865-4-6

Published and Printed in the United States of America

Dedication

Amidst the COVID-19 State of Emergency, my mother called me at 1 p.m. on April 4, 2020 and asked what I was doing. I told her I was writing my book. She asked, "How long have you been writing this book?" She laughed when I responded, "All my life."

"What's it about?" she asked. "Diversity and Inclusion," I responded, knowing that meant absolutely nothing to her. I set aside my pretentious airs and explained, "It's about my experiences of being black and a woman in my legal career and work situations. It's the type of book to help the reader understand and respect others from different races and backgrounds and hopefully, help make things better for everyone."

"Oh," she replied. She knew exactly what it meant. As the only woman of color, a divorced woman of lesser educational and financial means than her well-healed white counterparts, she sat in numerous high school events cheering me on through my social awkward book-nerdy years. She worked three jobs to fill in the gaps of the scholarships for the private college prep education that has afforded me the foundation for a future law career.

"Well, I hope you finish today, and dedicate it to me," she chuckled before she said goodbye.

So here it is: "Coffee and Conversations" dedicated to my mother, Gwendolyn Onita (Tensley) Beard.

Acknowledgements

Thank you to James, my husband, who brings me coffee or tea each morning in bed. He never forgets the honey. I appreciate our love, our daughters, and the extended family we have created.

Thank you to my friends, attorneys, and others who encouraged me to amplify my voice in the conversation of diversity and inclusion. Thank you to my Clan: Dorothy, Jane, and Sherry for the weekly call to keep my life and dreams on track. Thank you to all of the supportive and powerful women in my life: The ladies in my office (Jan, Jalona, and Jeannette), the Women With Wisdom and Courage, the Women Lawyers Association of Michigan especially Alena Clark, the National Association of the Negro Business and Professional Women's Clubs-Detroit Chapter (Lynda, Lois, Deanne, and Bar), the State Bar of Michigan Diversity and Inclusion Committee, the Detroit Bar Association, and the various Bar Associations who have trusted to me to write, chair a committee, and facilitate a training.

Thank you to God, who is the renowned artist of diversity and inclusion. She has been there all of my life and her word is the source of my inspiration. I am convinced that diversity and inclusion is the key to heaven on earth and gospel is to be shared over a cup of coffee.

Why Coffee and Conversations?

"In diversity there is beauty and there is strength."

~Maya Angelou

I clip the announcements from the Detroit Legal News announcing the appointments of Chief Diversity Officers, Directors of Inclusion and Equity. I send my LinkedIn colleagues and counterparts virtual high fives on their promotions and their articles. Diversity and inclusion are omnipresent in the legal community. The topics are on every conference and training agenda. The legal community is abuzz with enthusiasm and excitement for diversity, inclusion, and equity.

Diversity and inclusion are enjoying their moment in the spotlight. I have been privileged to sit on conference panels and podcasts and share ideas. But I have this gnawing feeling and am gathering evidence that I have experienced enough to know that we struggle to find how to fit them into our daily work lives. After the great conferences, annual diversity brunches, and symposiums, we return to business as usual. I can't let that happen.

Diversity and inclusion are not achieved with a single event or act. It is everyday occurrences that require attention and effort. Diversity and inclusion should be on our radar each day and discussed over coffee like the weather and sports. If diversity and inclusion topics infused our coffee conversations, people would really get to see and hear each other outside of a three day team building retreat, understand their daily impacts of differences, and perhaps widen their circle of associations and interactions by extending invitations to others who do not look like them, love like them, and worship like them.

When I write, I drink. My preferred coffee blend is a decaf medium roast, organic, brewed strongly with a big dollop of honey and an over pour of cream. As I write, I imagine myself sharing my experiences with you over a cup of coffee. I have drawn a mental composite of who you are. You are an attorney and we share a mutual interest in diversity and inclusion. However, we are not identical; maybe we are from different races, generations, genders, faiths, abilities, or politics. As your sister in the law and a certified diversity professional, I share the teachings and resources of diversity and inclusion applicable to our legal community and our justice system. As a black woman, I share my personal everyday experiences as one black woman's experience in our legal world.

I hope you invite me for coffee often. I hope you dog-ear pages of this book and write me with your thoughts on diversity and inclusion. We need every voice we can get in this conversation if we want sustaining conversation and meaningful impact. I dream that you purchase another copy of this book and leave it on someone's desk that is outside your regular coffee klatch with a yellow Post-it note inscribed "Thought of you. Let's grab some coffee and conversation."

"We should keep calm in the face of difference, and live our lives in a state of inclusion and wonder at the diversity of the humanity." ~George Takei

Ground Rules

My experience as mediator and diversity and inclusion facilitator require that I set ground rules before I get into the substance of a training conversation. Ground rules govern expectations and set boundaries, allowing me the opportunity to accomplish what I set out to do in an organized fashion. More importantly, it is an opportunity to get mutual agreement and commitment and establish how we will proceed to our destination.

Here are my ground rules and their definitions:

- Speak from My Own Experiences. Be frank and be brave. I have over five decades as a black woman, two decades as a black woman lawyer and court leader. Value my experiences and share so others can take them and learn.

"Although the world is full of suffering, it is full also of the overcoming of it." ~Helen Keller

- Honor Confidentiality. I've changed the names, unless I expressly received the permission of the person to use their name.

"When someone is comfortable enough to open up, share their thoughts, speak freely around you, don't ruin it by running your messy mouth." ~Unknown

- Expect to be uncomfortable. Being uncomfortable is part of the writing process, and is inherent in diversity and inclusion conversations. But as I'm not writing and speaking just for the sake of doing so, I am willing to be in the spaces where I do not have all the answers and perfection does not exist.

"Growth and comfort do not coexist." ~Ginni Rometty

- Respect. This applies in multiple ways. First, diversity and inclusion is a journey. Realize those who choose this journey may be on different paths and moving at different paces even when on the same path. Encourage everyone to move forward. Value the perspective of others. Do not pressure anyone to disclose more than they are willing to disclose. Remember abstractions such as professionalism mean different things to different people.

Respect as an action means listening. Avoid assumptions. Assumptions are worthless. Questions and apologies are important learning tools. Start with the best intent for yourself, others, and the situation. Use open-ended questions to gain understanding for the things you don't know and apologies for the things you get wrong and will not repeat.

"Would 'sorry' have made any difference? Does it ever? It's just a word. One word against a thousand actions." ~Sarah Ockler

The Year of Inclusion

I have proclaimed 2020 as *The Year of Inclusion*. I announced it on LinkedIn as an invitation for us to build inclusive workplaces in the legal community.

On January 19, 2020, I was the plenary speaker at diversity training for child support professionals and spoke on the workplace challenge of inclusion. Approximately 1 in every 4 children will be involved in the child support system.

Attorneys serve in the child support system as case workers, prosecutors, friends of the courts, and court administrators. There are 2,704 active members in the Michigan State Bar Family Law Section:

- Attorneys born 1944-1960 (Boomers) comprise 34% of the membership

- Attorneys born 1961-1980 (Gen X'ers) comprise 35% of the membership

- Europeans make up 81.2% of the membership

- African Americans make up 4.8% of the membership

- Men represent 52.4% of the membership and females represent 47.6% of the membership. (There is no other gender identifications listed.)

The plenary session was entitled *The Year of Inclusion*. It was a 45 minute primer to diversity and inclusion. Like many professionals, attorneys are questioning where they fit into the diversity conversation. Most can check off they are not racist, homophobic, or gender biased. Most feel they work well with others and treat each person they encounter with professionalism and respect.

For attorneys who question if or where they fit in the diversity conversation, start with inclusion. Inclusion is relevant to us as individuals and as attorneys who represent clients and organizations, serve in leadership capacities for local and national bar associations, and ascend to judgeship. Inclusion has a space for all of us.

Welcome to the Friend of the Court

Brené Brown's definition of belonging is "It's a practice that requires us to be vulnerable, get uncomfortable, and learn how to be present with people — without sacrificing who we are." When I first began at the Friend of the Court it was definitely not a place where I felt I belonged.

It was the little things. Within weeks of starting at the Friend of the Court, I was greeted by a floor supervisor. (A floor supervisor is someone responsible for the work of the department on the floor, but does not directly supervise everyone on the floor.) Let's call him "Chuck." Chuck was a white male, probably mid-30s, whom I had heard that, like me, had recently passed the bar. I was prepared for a perfunctory welcome--here's a little bit about our organization, and we are glad to have you. However, Chuck starts the conversation not only stating he is an attorney, but sharing his accomplishment of multi-stating. I acknowledged this great accomplishment and he proceeds to interject at least two more times in the brief encounter that he multi-stated on the bar exam. Finally, he pauses for what I interpreted as an invitation for me to share my scores as well. I plaster a polite smile on my face. My home training is that you do not share more than you have to, and you definitely don't share when strangers are making unusual and personal inquiries. Our conversation ends with the awkward silence, and him walking away. No "glad to have you" message. I made up my mind not to invest any time getting to know him.

I absolutely could not see myself working at the Wayne County Friend of the Court long-term. I continued to seek other employment. My job search resulted in many second interviews and call backs, but no offers. The Court's HR Department posted the opening for Friend of Court Attorney. Chuck stopped by on the pretense to shoot the breeze and just check on things. In a soliloquy, he reminded me that he multi-stated on the bar, and then began to enlighten me on how promotions worked.

"I will pass the test. Jackie will pass the test. She just finished law school. And Margo will pass. We will be promoted," he informed me as if he had the questions and answers for the exam and interview in his suit pocket.

Of course, his name would be number 1 on the list he said as casually as most people say the time of day. After all, he assured me, "People had to pay their dues."

As the only African American person eligible to apply for the opening, I read his message as a variation of that "Coloreds Need Not Apply" sign in a storefront window. I had mastered the plastered smile and nodded perfunctorily. Nothing fuels determination more than a challenge. I had nothing to lose, so I took the test. Then I prepped for the interview. Of course, being brought up on the adage that as a person of color you have to work twice as hard to get half as much, I studied long hours and thoroughly prepared. The gloves were off.

Ding. Ding. Round three with Chuck was a little different. Chuck showed up at my cubicle. He shared that he was past the exam and interview. I could not resist and finally repaid his courtesy, "I'm the top candidate." I promoted a few weeks before Chuck.

Back then I did not know about microaggressions. I leaned on common sense, like when Chuck waltzed to my cubicle and announced, "ZZ. I'm going to call you ZZ." Rather than removing my earrings, greasing up, and putting on the gloves to deliver a hell of a blow to the head, I replied, "No." No further discussion warranted. It was a lot easier to address Chuck as an equal than a subordinate. Grace, hard work, and karma never failed me.

Service Is Not Our Middle Name

As I stated, my initial goal was to leave this place as soon as possible. It was embedded in the culture. The second floor customer service window was the busy place in the organization. It was infamous. Each night the cleaning people had to wipe splattered, dried spit from both sides of the Plexiglas customer service window.

My job search went into overdrive after I had a particular training session at the customer service window. The trainer was assigned to show the new hires how to handle inquiries at the window. As the young woman approached, I smiled. She was a friendly face. My trainer asked her a question. That question led to another question and to another. The mechanics of child support are not easy, and the processes are complicated to the public. However, that may be not readily apparent to the staff who know the processes and have mastered the acronyms and legalese. I can't recall the specifics of any of the questions, but voices began rising on both sides. To end the interaction, my trainer offered to tag out and get his supervisor to continue the wrestling match. The woman gave up and left.

The woman called me later that evening at home. As I said, she was a friendly face; she had been my beautician for the past year and lived about two blocks from my home.

She asked, "What is wrong with that place?"

I confessed, "I don't have a clue. I'm trying to leave here as quickly as I can."

By the way, the woman's five-year-old-son had a terminable illness and he died about 18 months after her visit to the window. We need to treat each other with kindness as we do not know what others are going through.

The Intentionality of Inclusion

During my years with the Court, I have ascended the ranks and have taken on roles with increasing responsibility. I belong and it is my responsibility to ensure that others have that experience. I have welcomed new hires, telling them to avoid naysayers and to help develop what they want to see in the workplace. I have been in coffee klatches with colleagues to share networking and discuss promotional opportunities and met new hires for coffee to encourage and mentor their professional development. I have shared what I know with black, white, male, female, gay, lawyers, social workers, support court staff, and others. We find a break time of lunch hour to talk. I am proud when each finds their dream job, whether it is in the court or elsewhere.

As for the public, I created the outreach initiative Friend of the Court For Our Children in 2006. It started out as volunteer after-hours work with a colleague/friend. It has grown to include a bench warrant amnesty project, a semi-annual library event to serve the public, and several outreaches in communities. Today, the program is still in capable hands and continues to grow to include services in the Hispanic and Arabic-American community. Annual public satisfaction surveys also allow us to find where we may improve our delivery of services.

We must be intentional and deliberate to create inclusiveness. Our established routines and habits can be barriers to creating inclusiveness.

Since 1972, the Third Circuit Court has hosted a visiting judge from Japan. It's called the Japanese Judge Program. In 2015, as Court Administrator, I received a letter from the Supreme Court of Japan announcing the visiting judge for the year. Here's the routine: My office makes arrangements for the judge to visit the divisions of the court and we check in with him about once per quarter. This was the established routine I inherited and it was easy to follow. When the General Counsel's office notified me that they no longer had an office available for the visiting judge, I stopped and assessed how little my office interacted with the judge.

The visiting judge leaves his family and his home court. He travels from Tokyo, Japan to Detroit, which is over 6,000 miles as the crow flies to come learn about our court and its tradition. I probably spent less than an 8 hour workday equivalent with him.

"How could I be a better hostess? Was it even appropriate to refer the judge as the Japan Judge?" I asked myself. If someone referred to me as the Black Court Administrator, I would question their motives.

My assignment was to not find the Judge from Japan an office somewhere; I had space within my suite to create him an office. He would sit with us and be in the suite with the Chief Judge. Since then, my office staff and I have been blessed to meet and get to know the visiting judges from Japan.

One Judge even told me it was okay to say "Japanese Judge"; however, it still did not sit well with me, so I still say visiting Judge from Japan.

We have celebrated birthdays, learned about their families, shared meals, failed to get out of the Escape Room, attended bar events, eaten snacks, and exchanged gifts. Getting to know each other helped eliminate the stereotypes. Eminem's movie "8 Mile" is well known in Japan and is accepted as a representation of modern downtown Detroit.

I'm glad that I took the time to become more intentional in hosting our international guests. We were recently notified that the Visiting Judge program is being suspended and our most recent visitor is leaving early because of the pandemic.

"It's important to create space for those of us who are made to feel as though we don't belong or that we're not good enough – because the truth is, we do, and we are." ~Morgan DeBaun, Founder & CEO of Blavity

Lessons Learned

1. People want to have a sense of belonging.

2. We have all be in a group; we have all felt left out, and that we did not belong.

3. Our exclusionary actions may be unintentional.

4. Established routines can be barriers to creating inclusion.

Coffee Conversations Discussion Questions:

- How have you been left out in the workplace?

- Who have you excluded in the workplace?

- How can you make the workplace more inclusive?

Finish this statement: Workplace inclusion is the smile that greets you, the handshake that welcomes you, and _____.

Best practices:

1. Be intentional.

2. Look at everyday situations from new perspectives and discover additional ways you may be inclusive.

3. Review established routines to ensure you have not overlooked opportunities to be inclusive.

4. Welcome others from different social identities and cultures to work.

5. Invite people with different social identities to meetings, lunches, and to grab a cup of

coffee. Ask them how they are doing to identify ways you can welcome them into the work environment.

6. Ask your customers how is your service?

Bonus:

I have two bonuses for you.

First, the most powerful message on inclusion is a YouTube video that has images and only music. "Inclusion Starts With I."

Second, visiting the National S.E.E.D project was helpful. The goal of the nine month training is to "create conversational community that drives change." If there is a session in your neighborhood, sign up for it.

Email me at Zenell@allinspiringminds.com to share your experience.

Upcoming *Coffee and Conversations: Pipelines, Bridges, and Pathways to Diversity and Inclusion*

Whether or not we create a diverse and inclusive legal community depends to a great degree on the response from those who sit in places of leadership. In the legal profession, the bulk of leadership remains in the hands of white men. According to the State Bar of Michigan in 2019, over 85% of the bar was male and European. It usually takes years of experience to gain expertise and status in a profession, and the data indicates that older white men would hold that ranking as well. To impact change, we need white men with power, influence, and success to be at the table to discuss how power, influence, and success can be inclusive.

But I have asked myself, "Why would they accept the invitation?"

Appendix

The 2019 State Bar of Michigan Statewide Demographics publication reports that there are 35,360 active Michigan residents who are members in the bar.

- Of the 35,337 who responded, 22,930 are male and 12,407 are female
- Of the 35,360 who responded:
  - 5.9% were born prior to 1944 (Traditionalists)
  - 34.3% were born 1944-1960 (Boomers)
  - 39% of the members were born in 1961-1980 (Gen X'ers)
  - 20.2% are born after 1981 (Millennials)
- Of the 24,809 who responded:
  - 81.7% identified their race/ethnicity as European
  - 5.7% as African American
  - 2.2% as Arab Origin
  - 2.1% as Asian-Pacific Islanders
  - 1.8% as Multi-Racial
  - 1.7% as Hispanic-Latino
  - 4.3% as Other

Thank you for your support. Please share your thoughts and feedback with the author at Zenell@allinspiringminds.com